An Animal Family

DUCKS AND DUCKLINGS

By Natalie Humphrey

Gareth Stevens PUBLISHING

Please visit our website, www.garethstevens.com. For a free color catalog of all our high-quality books, call toll free 1-800-542-2595 or fax 1-877-542-2596.

Library of Congress Cataloging-in-Publication Data

Names: Humphrey, Natalie, author.
Title: Ducks and ducklings / Natalie Humphrey.
Description: New York : Gareth Stevens Publishing, [2021] | Series: An animal family | Includes index.
Identifiers: LCCN 2019044948 | ISBN 9781538255889 (library binding) | ISBN 9781538255865 (paperback) | ISBN 9781538255872 | ISBN 9781538255896 (ebook)
Subjects: LCSH: Ducklings–Juvenile literature. | Ducks–Development–Juvenile literature.
Classification: LCC QL696.A52 H845 2021 | DDC 598.4/1–dc23
LC record available at https://lccn.loc.gov/2019044948

First Edition

Published in 2021 by
Gareth Stevens Publishing
111 East 14th Street, Suite 349
New York, NY 10003

Editor: Natalie Humphrey
Designer: Katelyn E. Reynolds

Photo credits: Cover, p. 1 CreativeMedia.org.uk/Shutterstock.com; p. 5 KACHALKIN OLEG/Shutterstock.com; pp. 7, 24 (egg) sahua d/Shutterstock.com; pp. 9, 24 (nest) bepin/Shutterstock.com; p. 11 Digital Zoo/DigitalVision/Getty Images; p. 13 5 second Studio/Shutterstock.com; p. 15 Sheila Fitzgerald/Shutterstock.com; p. 17 shaftinaction/Shutterstock.com; p. 19 Jordi Jornet/Shutterstock.com; pp. 21, 24 (flock) Marcia Straub/Moment/Getty Images; p. 23 Inna G/Shutterstock.com.

Printed in the United States of America

CPSIA compliance information: Batch #CS20GS: For further information contact Gareth Stevens, New York, New York at 1-800-542-2595.

Contents

Mother ducks make nests. They make them by water.

They lay 8 eggs
in their nests.
They can lay 13!

Mothers sit on their nests.

Ducklings come from the eggs.

They are very fuzzy.

Ducklings follow their mother.

They eat bugs
and plants.

They grow up in two months!

Grown ducks live in flocks.

They start families too!

Words to Know

egg

flock

nest

Index